TRANSFORM YOUR LIFE IN 30 DAYS

Simple Habits for Lasting Happiness and Success

Author:

Michel Fredericks

Editor: World Vision

Copyright@2023

TABLE OF CONTENTS

CHAPTER 1
Introduction

CHAPTER 2
The Power of Habits

CHAPTER 3
The 30-Day Challenge

CHAPTER 4
Simple Habits for Transformation

Habits for Lasting Happiness and Success

CHAPTER 5
Implementing and Tracking Habits

CHAPTER 6
Overcoming Obstacles

CHAPTER 7
Reflecting on Progress

CHAPTER 8
Conclusion

Study Guide

CHAPTER 1

Introduction

Are you looking for a way to improve your life and achieve lasting happiness and success? If so, "Transform Your Life in 30 Days: Simple Habits for Lasting Happiness and Success" is the book for you. This comprehensive guide is designed to help readers make significant changes in their lives in just 30 days by introducing them to simple and practical habits that will promote happiness and success.

In today's fast-paced world, it can take time to find time to focus on personal growth and development. However, with this book, you'll learn that small changes in your daily routine can significantly impact your overall well-being. The book aims to provide readers with practical and actionable advice they can apply immediately.

The Importance of Developing Habits

Habits are powerful tools that shape our lives and determine our success. They are automatic and unconscious behaviors that we repeat daily, and over time, they become deeply ingrained in our psyche. Habits can be positive or negative, and it's crucial to identify the ones holding us back and replace them with new, more beneficial ones.

Positive habits significantly impact our happiness and success and are the key to transforming our lives. By developing positive habits, we can achieve our goals, improve our relationships, increase our confidence and self-esteem, and experience a sense of purpose and fulfillment.

This book will explore the essential habits for lasting happiness and success and show you how to incorporate them into your daily routine. Whether you're looking to improve your health, relationships, career, or financial situation, this book provides the tools and guidance you need to achieve your goals.

The 30-Day Challenge

"Transform Your Life in 30 Days" is structured as a 30-day challenge, each day focused on a different habit. Each chapter comprehensively explains the practice, why it's essential, and how to implement it. The book also includes practical tips, exercises, and journal prompts to help you integrate the habit into your daily routine and make it a permanent part of your life.

By the end of the 30 days, you'll have established 30 new habits that will dramatically improve your life and help you achieve your goals. You'll experience a sense of accomplishment and pride and be well on creating a life you love.

CHAPTER 2

The Power of Habits

Habits play a crucial role in our lives and profoundly impact our well-being. They shape our behavior, thoughts, and emotions and determine our success and happiness. Understanding the science of habits and how they work is essential for creating positive ones and breaking negative ones.

Psychologists and neuroscientists have extensively studied the science of habits and have uncovered some fascinating insights into how patterns work. Habits are formed when our brains associate a particular behavior with a specific cue or context. Over time, the behavior becomes automatic and unconscious, becoming a habit.

The habit loop consists of three parts: a cue, a routine, and a reward. The signal triggers the habit, and the performance is the following behavior. The bonus reinforces the practice and makes it more likely to continue. By understanding the habit loop, we can identify the cues that trigger our habits and replace harmful routines with positive ones.

Creating Positive Habits

Positive habits significantly impact our happiness and success and are the key to transforming our lives. They are the behaviors we repeat daily, and over time, they become deeply ingrained in our psyche. Positive habits can help us achieve our goals, improve our relationships, increase our confidence and self-esteem, and experience a sense of purpose and fulfillment.

However, creating positive habits can be challenging. It takes time, effort, and discipline to establish new behaviors and make them a permanent part of our lives. But with the right tools and strategies, anyone can create positive habits and reap the benefits.

One effective way to create positive habits is to make them small and achievable. Starting with small changes can help us build momentum and establish the routine. It's also essential to be consistent and persistent, as habits take time to form, and it's necessary to stick with them even when progress is slow.

Breaking Negative Habits

Damaging habits can hold us back and prevent us from achieving our goals. They are behaviors that are detrimental to our well-being and keep us from living the life we want. Damaging habits can profoundly impact our lives, whether procrastination, overeating, smoking, or other harmful behavior.

Breaking negative habits requires a different approach than creating positive ones. Identifying the cues that trigger the addiction and replacing the negative routine with a positive one is essential.

This can be challenging, as practices are deeply ingrained in our psyche, and breaking them takes time and effort.

Another effective strategy for breaking negative habits is to enlist the support of friends, family, or a therapist. Someone holding us accountable and providing encouragement and support can be essential for breaking negative habits.

CHAPTER 3

The 30-Day Challenge

The 30-Day challenge is a transformative process that involves adopting one new habit every day for 30 days. This challenge aims to help individuals create lasting change in their lives by establishing positive habits and breaking negative ones. By adopting a new daily routine, individuals can gradually develop a foundation of positive habits that will support them in creating the life they desire.

Whether you're looking to improve your health, relationships, career, or financial situation, the 30-day challenge provides a structured and accountable way to create lasting change. The challenge is designed to be simple yet powerful, and by the end of the 30 days, individuals will have established 30 new positive habits that will transform their lives in ways they never thought possible.

So, if you're ready to take the challenge and start transforming your life, grab a journal, choose your habits, and get ready to begin the journey of a lifetime.

Here is a sample list of exercises that could be taken every day for 30 days, covering various aspects of personal growth and development, including spiritual, mental, educational, and physical health and more:

Day 1: Practice Gratitude

Start your day by reflecting on three things you are grateful for. For example, you might be thankful for your health, the roof over your head, or the support of your loved ones. This simple exercise can help shift your focus from what's lacking in your life to what you already have, which can improve your overall mood and increase feelings of happiness and contentment.

Day 2: Meditation

Take ten minutes to quiet your mind and focus on your breath. Meditation has been shown to reduce stress, improve focus, and enhance emotional well-being. You can use guided meditations or find a quiet space and focus on your breath.

Day 3: Read for Knowledge

Spend 30 minutes reading on a topic that interests you, whether it's a novel, a self-help book, or an article on a subject you'd like to learn more about. The goal is to stimulate your mind and expand your knowledge base.

Day 4: Exercise

Exercise has improved physical health, boost mood, and reduced stress. Make physical activity a part of your daily routine by dedicating 30 minutes to exercise. This can be anything from running, yoga, or walking.

Day 5: Self-Care

Take time for yourself to recharge and refresh. This might involve taking a relaxing bath, getting a massage, or taking a nap. By prioritizing self-care, you'll be able to perform at your best in all aspects of your life.

Day 6: Declutter

Tackle the clutter in your home or workspace by removing items you no longer need or use. Decluttering can help reduce stress and increase productivity by creating a more organized and harmonious environment.

Day 7: Connect with Loved Ones

Reach out to a friend or loved one and spent time connecting and catching up. Relationships play a crucial role in our overall well-being, so nurturing these connections is essential.

Day 8: Positive Self-Talk

Practice speaking kindly to yourself and reframing negative thoughts with positive ones. For example, instead of saying, "I'm such a failure," try saying, "I'm doing my best, and that's enough." This can help improve self-esteem and confidence and reduce feelings of stress and anxiety.

Day 9: Give Back

Volunteer at a local charity, perform a random act of kindness or offer a helping hand to someone in need. By giving back, you'll not only make a positive impact on the world, but you'll also improve your emotional well-being.

Day 10: Healthy Eating

Try a new healthy recipe or make a conscious effort to eat more nutritious foods. Good nutrition is critical to maintaining physical health, and trying new healthy recipes can help broaden your culinary horizons and make healthy eating more enjoyable.

Day 11: Creativity

Engage in creative activities, such as painting, drawing, or writing. Creativity has been shown to boost mood, reduce stress, and improve overall well-being.

Day 12: Reflection and Goal-Setting

Reflect on your progress so far and set new goals for the future. This could involve making a vision board, writing down your goals, or simply thinking about what you want to achieve.

Day 13: Nature

Get outside and spend time in nature, whether for a hike, gardening, or simply walking. Spending time in nature has been shown to improve physical health, reduce stress, and enhance overall well-being.

14: Journaling

Take ten minutes to write in a journal about your thoughts, feelings, and experiences. Journaling can help reduce stress, promote self-reflection, and provide a means of expressing and processing emotions.

Day 15: Mindfulness

Practice mindfulness by focusing on the present moment and letting go of distractions. This can be done through mindfulness exercises such as deep breathing or simply paying attention to your surroundings.

Day 16: Sleep

Make a concerted effort to get at least seven hours of sleep each night. Sleep plays a crucial role in physical and emotional well-being and can help reduce stress and improve focus and productivity.

Day 17: Limit Screen Time

Try to limit your time spent on screens, such as televisions, computers, and smartphones, to up to two hours per day. Excessive screen time has been linked to poor sleep, eye strain, and other health problems.

Day 18: Affirmations

Repeat positive affirmations to yourself each day, such as "I am worthy and deserving of happiness and success." Affirmations can help boost self-esteem, reduce stress, and improve overall well-being.

Day 19: Gratitude Letter

Write a gratitude letter to someone who has positively impacted your life, expressing your appreciation and gratitude. Expressing gratitude has been shown to improve emotional well-being and strengthen relationships.

Day 20: Relaxation

Practice relaxation techniques like deep breathing, progressive muscle relaxation, or visualization. Relaxation can help reduce stress, improve sleep, and promote overall well-being.

Day 21: Learning a New Skill

Spend 30 minutes each day learning a new skill, such as a new language, a musical instrument, or a recipe. Learning new skills can help improve cognitive function, boost mood, and reduce stress.

Day 22: Emotional Intelligence

Practice empathy and active listening, making an effort to understand others' perspectives and emotions. Emotional intelligence can help improve relationships, reduce stress, and enhance overall well-being.

Day 23: Water

Drink at least eight glasses of water daily to stay hydrated and maintain physical health. Proper hydration has been shown to improve energy levels, boost mood, and enhance cognitive function.

Day 24: Forgiveness

Practice forgiveness by letting go of grudges and negative feelings towards others. Forgiveness has been shown to reduce stress, improve emotional well-being, and enhance relationships.

Day 25: Decline Negative Thoughts

Practice declining negative thoughts by reframing them in a positive light or simply letting them go. This can help reduce stress, improve mood, and enhance overall well-being.

Day 26: Yoga

Practice yoga to improve physical health, reduce stress, and enhance overall well-being. Even just 10-15 minutes of yoga each day can make a positive impact.

Day 27: Gratitude Jar

Start a gratitude jar and write down what you are thankful for daily. Revisit your gratitude jar often to reflect on all the positive things in your life.

Day 28: Simplify

Simplify your life by decluttering, downsizing, and letting go of excess possessions. Simplifying can help reduce stress, increase productivity, and enhance overall well-being.

Day 29: Volunteer

Volunteer at a local charity, community center, or other organization to give back and positively impact. Volunteering can improve emotional well-being, reduce stress, and enhance overall well-being.

Day 30: Reflect and Celebrate

Reflect on your progress over the past 30 days and celebrate your successes. Take time to acknowledge your growth and celebrate all the positive changes you've made.

It is important to remember that the habits you choose should align with your goals and aspirations and should be focused on creating positive change in your life. The key is to start small and gradually increase the difficulty of the habits as the challenge progresses. With this in mind, feel free to modify this list to suit your needs and goals, and most importantly, enjoy the journey of self-discovery and transformation.

CHAPTER 4

Simple Habits for Transformation

Incorporating simple habits into your daily routine can profoundly impact your overall happiness and success. Here are a few examples of simple practices that you can adopt to transform your life:

1. **Gratitude** - Incorporating gratitude into your daily routine can significantly impact your happiness and success. Practicing gratitude helps shift your focus to the positive aspects of your life and can improve your overall outlook. Start each day by writing down three things you are grateful for and reflect on them throughout the day.

2. **Exercise** - Exercise is an essential habit for maintaining physical and emotional health. Exercise can reduce stress, boost mood, and improve cognitive function. Aim to get at least 30 minutes of moderate physical activity each day, whether through a workout, a walk, or simply stretching.

3. **Mindfulness** - Mindfulness is being present at the moment and focusing on your thoughts and emotions. Incorporating mindfulness into your daily routine can help reduce stress, improve emotional intelligence, and enhance overall well-being. You can practice

mindfulness through meditation, deep breathing exercises, or simply paying attention to your surroundings.

4. **Goal-Setting** - Setting goals is a powerful habit that can help you stay focused and motivated. Start by setting realistic and achievable goals in various areas, such as your career, relationships, and personal development. Regularly review and adjust your goals as necessary to ensure that you are making progress and staying on track.

5. **Self-Care** - Self-care is an essential habit for maintaining physical and emotional health. Make time each day to do something that nourishes you, whether reading a book, taking a bath, or simply taking a walk in nature. Prioritizing self-care helps reduce stress, improve mood, and enhance overall well-being.

6. **Organizational Skills** - Organizational skills can help reduce stress and increase productivity. Start by simplifying your workspace and establishing a routine for completing tasks. Keeping a to-do list, prioritizing tasks, and delegating responsibilities can help you stay organized and on track.

7. **Positive Affirmations** - Repeat positive affirmations to yourself daily to boost self-esteem, reduce stress, and improve overall

well-being. Positive affirmations help shift your focus to the positive aspects of your life and reinforce a growth mindset.

By incorporating these simple habits into your daily routine, you can transform your life in meaningful ways and set yourself on the path to lasting happiness and success.

Habits For Lasting Happiness and Success

Habits are the building blocks of our lives, shaping who we are and determining our level of happiness and success. It's important to cultivate positive habits that support our well-being and growth. Here are some habits that can help you achieve your goals and lead a fulfilling life:

1. Practice Gratitude: Fostering an attitude of gratitude can help you focus on the positive aspects of your life rather than dwelling on the negatives. Make it a habit to reflect on what you are thankful for each day, no matter how small the things may seem.

2. Exercise Regularly: Regular exercise has been shown to have numerous physical and mental health benefits. It can help reduce stress, improve mood, and increase energy levels. Make time for daily physical activity, whether running, practicing yoga, or simply taking a walk.

3. Cultivate Mindfulness: Mindfulness is fully present at the moment, without judgment.

You can start by paying attention to your breath for a few minutes each day. By being mindful, you can better understand your thoughts and emotions and improve your ability to cope with stress.

4. Surround Yourself with Positive People: The people you surround yourself with can significantly impact your well-being and success. Make it a habit to seek out positive and supportive relationships, and avoid toxic individuals who bring negativity into your life.

5. Set and Pursue Goals: Setting goals gives you direction and purpose, and pursuing them can help you feel more fulfilled and successful. Make sure your goals are realistic, achievable, and aligned with your values. Celebrate your progress along the way, and don't be discouraged by setbacks.

6. Practice Self-Care: Taking care of yourself is crucial for your physical and mental health. Make time for activities that bring you joy and relaxation, such as reading, practicing a hobby, or simply spending time in nature.

Your Brain and Happiness

The purpose of your brain is not to make you happy. Your brain is vital to your survival. Dopamine enhances positive emotions. When it reaches the brain's pleasure centers, it makes you feel good. When you complete a task, exercise, etc., you experience this "high."

Dopamine can now be manufactured to be released on its own. Previously, it was released as a means of survival. Due to our social environment, however, it can be made to emerge on its own. When you receive a message alert, you want to read it and determine who sent it. This keeps you in constant contact and on your phone. You are unknowingly causing dopamine to maintain your connection. Marketers have learned how to use dopamine to sell products and services in the modern world. This has caused us to become hooked. However, it is not necessary to act every time dopamine is released.

You are not required to check your phone when it notifies you. When dopamine is frequently activated, it can be harmful to the mind and body. This is how individuals remain addicted. Self-stimulation of the brain's pleasure centers may be advantageous but not happiness. People should not choose to feel better by overeating or engaging in other negative behaviors. This implies that you have lost control over your emotions. When you arrive, you will be unhappy. After the "high" wears off, your happiness will return to normal. 50% of our happiness is determined by our genes, 40% by internal factors, and 10% by external factors, according to research. Thus, it is clear that what occurs to you is less critical to your happiness than how you respond to it.

The Composition of Emotions

When you understand how your emotions function, you can manage them effectively. It is essential to remember that feelings change over time. They are not durable. They are traveling. If you take this approach, you will be in the best position to work with them.

Allow yourself to experience your emotions without adding anything to them. By including these notes, you can discover a deeper meaning that would not otherwise be apparent. No matter how hard you try, you cannot always be happy or sad. Avoid doing that. At various times in your life, you will experience different emotions. Place less reliance on them. The way we feel changes over time.

Your Negative Emotions Are Neither Incorrect Nor Useless. Negative emotions are not destructive, contrary to popular belief. As you progress through life, you may require them. They facilitate comprehension and make sense of things. Not having negative emotions is not inherently harmful. It's that you continue to dwell on them and punish yourself for them.

Positive outcomes that can result from negative emotions Without negative emotions, it is impossible to grow. Calm seas make no skilled sailor. These negative emotions aid in your recovery, which is a good thing. How rapidly emotions change, This is an excellent way to think about emotions, particularly negative ones. It makes it more obvious that whatever you are experiencing will not last forever. You can recall the negative feelings you participated in the past. Consider how you are better off now than you were previously. This is how emotions function. Your sorrow and suffering will pass; they will not always exist. But if you consistently feel the same, you must change your life. If your depression lasts for an extended period, you should speak with a counselor.

How challenging emotions can be

Observe how awful everything appears when you're going through a difficult time and how suddenly beautiful everything appears when you're experiencing a good time. It would be best if you remembered that you are not your emotions, nor are your feelings yours. You cannot always overcome your feelings, even if you are aware of this. We hope that your response will be more effective than in the past.

The Influence of Emotions

Emotions attract individuals like a magnet. If you are in a good mood, other positive emotions will follow. If you feel bad, you will attract more negative circumstances into your life. Your thoughts are composed of your feelings, and your feelings are composed of your thoughts. It is like a loop. Here's

How to Escape from It

It would be best if you learned to keep your emotions separate. Place each in a separate box and prevent them from touching. This allows you to concentrate on a limited number of tasks simultaneously. Ask yourself specific questions and provide honest answers.

- What caused the feeling to occur?
- What caused the rate to increase?
- What type of narrative did you tell yourself?
- Why and how did you begin walking again?

How Easily You Can Feel

If you feel good, you are more likely to have positive thoughts. Similarly, if you are experiencing negative emotions, you are more likely to have negative thoughts. It is difficult to transition from a positive to a negative state.

Your emotional set point When you're feeling bad, you should always seek out stronger emotions. You could maximize this opportunity. This would pull you toward the good. Among the symptoms of depression, anger ranks first. Being angry requires more energy than being sad.

When you become angry, you may be mad at yourself for being who you are. You quickly become angry with yourself for being angry. You could " resolve" your problems by ascending. So, anger is essential to getting you out of a bad mood and into a good one. Painful feelings and thoughts When you have negative emotions, you often cause yourself internal suffering. When in such a predicament, all you can think about is how to make matters worse for yourself.

Thoughts such as:

1. What will happen if this pain doesn't stop?
2. What if I never make enough money to care for my family and myself?

These questions provide no solution to your problems. They only bring you suffering. The issue is not necessarily the negative emotions you experience when asking such questions. The point is the mental suffering you inflict upon yourself.

1. Why There Are No Concerns
2. When you examine your problem from a different perspective, you realize it does not exist.

What you do not acknowledge does not exist. When you consider a problem, it becomes apparent.

Problems occur over time. If you consider the past or future, you are not considering time.

For a problem to exist, it must be identified as such: if you do not perceive something as a problem, it does not exist.

We misunderstand it, which is the issue.

Using your body to change how you feel

Your body is a potent tool for shaping your emotions and thoughts. By making simple yet intentional changes to your posture, movement, and breathing, you can immediately alter how you feel physically and mentally. Here are a few creative examples to get you started:

1. Stand tall and proud: When you stand tall with your shoulders back and chest out, you automatically create a sense of confidence and power. This simple adjustment can help you feel more assertive and capable, even when facing challenges or tough decisions.

2. Take a deep breath: Deep breathing is a simple yet effective way to calm the mind and reduce stress. Focus on the sensation of the air moving in and out of your body, and let any worries or distractions drift away. Next time you feel overwhelmed, try closing your eyes and taking three deep breaths.

3. Smile and make a silly face: Smiling and laughing have been shown to affect our mood and emotions positively. So, next time you're feeling down, try making a stupid face or smiling for a full minute. The physical act of

smiling sends signals to your brain that it's time to be happy.

4. Dance it out: Movement is a great way to release pent-up energy and emotions. Put on your favorite song and let yourself dance freely, allowing your body to express how you feel in the moment. You'll be amazed at how much better you feel after just a few minutes of movement.

5. Stretch and release tension: When we hold tension in our bodies, it can contribute to feelings of stress and anxiety. Pay attention to the sensation of your muscles relaxing and let go of any negative thoughts or feelings. Take a few minutes to stretch and release any tension you may be having.

By using your body to change your emotions and thoughts, you tap into the mind-body connection, which has been shown to have a powerful impact on our overall well-being. So, get creative and see what works best for you!

Letting Your Thoughts Affect How You Feel

Just as your body can affect how you feel, your thoughts and beliefs can also significantly shape your emotions. Here are a few creative examples to show you how:

1. Reframe your thoughts: How you interpret events and experiences can significantly impact how you feel. Instead of focusing on

the negative, try to look for the positive in each situation and reframe your thoughts accordingly. For example, if you're feeling overwhelmed, remind yourself of everything you have accomplished and the skills you bring to the table.

2. Practice gratitude: Focusing on what you're thankful for can help shift your focus away from negative thoughts and emotions. Try writing down three things you're grateful for each day, no matter how small they may seem. This simple act can help you cultivate a more positive outlook on life.

3. Use positive affirmations: Positive affirmations are powerful statements that help to reframe negative beliefs and reinforce positive ones. Repeat affirmations that resonate with you, such as "I am worthy and deserving of happiness" or "I am capable and strong." The more you repeat these affirmations, the more they'll become a part of your belief system.

4. Surround yourself with positive influences: The people you surround yourself with can significantly impact how you feel. Try to spend time with people who support and encourage you, and distance yourself from those who bring you down.

5. Please focus on the present moment: When we get lost in our thoughts, it's easy to get caught

up in worry and stress. Try to focus on the present moment, taking in your surroundings and noticing the sensations in your body. This can help you stay grounded and centered, even facing challenges.

By letting your thoughts affect how you feel, you tap into the power of the mind-body connection and can create a positive, resilient mindset. So, try incorporating these techniques into your daily routine and see their impact on your well-being.

Using Your Words to Change How You Feel

Words have the power to shape our thoughts, emotions, and beliefs. By choosing the words we use carefully and speaking them with intention, we can positively impact how we feel. Here are a few creative examples to inspire you:

1. Use empowering language: The words we use can either empower or disempower us. Choose to use language that makes you feel strong, confident, and capable. For example, instead of saying, "I can't do this," try saying, "I'm figuring this out."

2. Speak kind words to yourself: We often speak to ourselves in a way that we wouldn't talk to others. Try to be kind and gentle with yourself, using words of encouragement and support. Repeat affirmations that make you feel good, such as "I am capable and deserving of happiness."

3. Reframe negative experiences: When faced with challenges, it can be easy to get caught up in negative thoughts and emotions. Instead of dwelling on what's gone wrong, try to reframe the experience in a positive light. Focus on what you learned and how you can grow from the situation.

4. Use the power of visualization: A visualization is a powerful tool for shaping our emotions and beliefs. Close your eyes and imagine yourself in a positive, happy state. Repeat positive affirmations to yourself and let the words sink in.

5. Please share your thoughts and feelings with others: Talking about our experiences and emotions can help us process and make sense of them. Find someone you trust and share how you're feeling. The act of speaking your truth can be incredibly empowering and healing.

By using your words to change how you feel, you tap into the power of the mind-body connection and can create a positive, resilient mindset. So, choose your words wisely and use them to create the life you want.

Ways In Which Your Environment Affects How You Feel

The environment we surround ourselves with can significantly impact our mood and well-being. Here are a few ways in which our environment affects how we feel:

1. Light: Exposure to natural light has improved mood, boosted energy levels, and promoted overall well-being. On the other hand, lack of sunlight can contribute to sadness, fatigue, and depression.

2. Color: The colors we surround ourselves with can also impact our emotions. Bright, bold colors can energize and invigorate, while soft, muted colors can create a sense of calm and tranquility.

3. Nature: Spending time in nature has improved mood, reduced stress levels, and increased happiness and well-being. Even just a few minutes spent outside can have a positive impact.

4. Clutter: Clutter in the environment can create stress, anxiety, and overwhelm. Keeping your living and work spaces organized and free of clutter can help you feel calmer and more focused.

5. Noise: Excessive noise can contribute to stress and anxiety, while soft, calming sounds like white noise can have a relaxing effect.

6. Aromas: Certain scents have been shown to have a powerful impact on our emotions. For example, the smell of lavender has been shown to have a calming effect, while the scent of citrus can energize and uplift.

By being mindful of the environment around you and making minor changes to create a more positive space, you can significantly impact how you feel. So, pay attention to the sights, sounds, and sensations in your environment, and make changes as needed to create a space that supports and uplifts you.

How Music Affects Your Emotions

Music profoundly impacts our emotions, evoking joy, sadness, excitement, and more. Here are a few ways in which music can affect our emotions:

1. Tempo: The tempo, or speed, of a piece of music can significantly impact how it makes us feel. Fast-paced, energetic music can make us more awake and alert, while slow, soothing music can help us relax and unwind.

2. Melody: The melody, or tune, of a piece of music can evoke a range of emotions, from joyful to sad and contemplative. Listening to music with a song that aligns with your current mood can help you tap into and enhance those feelings.

3. Lyrics: The lyrics of a song can also have a powerful impact on our emotions. Listening to music with lyrics that speak to our

experiences and emotions can help us process and make sense of those feelings.

4. Association: Our emotions can also be affected by our associations with certain songs or artists. For example, hearing a popular piece during a particularly happy or significant time in our lives can bring back feelings of joy and nostalgia.

5. Culture and context: Music can also be culturally and contextually tied to emotions. For example, listening to a traditional folk song from a specific region may evoke feelings of pride and connection to one's cultural heritage.

Music can touch us on a deep emotional level and evoke feelings and memories that may have been long forgotten. So, choose your musical selections carefully and let the power of music shape and enhance your emotions.

How Emotions Are Formed

Emotions are complex and multi-faceted experiences that are formed through the interaction of several factors. Here is a general overview of how emotions are created:

1. Stimulus: The first step in forming emotions is the presence of a catalyst. This can be anything from a person, object, event, or thought that elicits a response in us.

2. Perception: Our perception of the stimulus is critical in how we experience emotions. Our perception is shaped by our previous experiences, beliefs, and expectations and can influence how we respond to the stimulus.

3. Cognitive appraisal: Once we've perceived the stimulus, our brain then evaluates the situation through a process known as cognitive appraisal. This process helps us determine the significance of the inspiration and the appropriate response.

4. Physiological response: Our body also responds to the stimulus, releasing chemicals and hormones like adrenaline, cortisol, and oxytocin that prepare us for action. These physiological responses play a role in shaping our emotions.

5. Emotional experience: The final step in forming emotions is the experience of the emotion itself. The stimulus, perception, cognitive appraisal, and physiological response influence this subjective experience.

Emotions are complex and dynamic, shaped by various internal and external factors. By understanding how emotions are formed, we can gain insight into our emotional experiences and work towards managing and regulating them healthily and adaptively.

Ways To Change How You Understand Something

Changing how we understand something can be a powerful learning and personal growth tool. Here are a few ways to change how you know something:

1. Get multiple perspectives: Gaining various perspectives on a topic can help broaden your understanding and challenge your preconceived notions. This can include seeking out information from diverse sources, talking to people with different experiences and perspectives, and actively seeking dissenting views.

2. Reframe the problem: Reframing how you think about a situation can help you see it from a different angle and find new solutions. For example, instead of thinking of a challenge as an obstacle, try seeing it as an opportunity for growth.

3. Practice active listening: Active listening involves being fully present and engaged when someone is speaking, paying close attention to their words and body language. You can gain a deeper understanding of their perspectives and experiences by actively listening to others.

4. Ask questions: Asking questions can help you clarify your understanding and gain new insights. When you ask open-ended questions,

you allow others to share their thoughts and experiences, which can broaden your knowledge.

5. Seek out new experiences: Experiencing something new can challenge your beliefs and broaden your understanding. This can include trying new activities, traveling to new places, and stepping outside your comfort zone.

6. Reflect on your experiences: Taking the time to reflect on your experiences can help you better understand yourself and your place in the world. This can involve journaling, meditating, or self-reflection through conversation with a trusted friend or therapist.

Using these strategies, you can expand your understanding and cultivate a more holistic, nuanced perspective on the world around you.

Solution To Deal with Negative Emotion Short and Long Term

Dealing with negative emotions can be challenging, but short-term and long-term solutions can help.

Short-term solutions:

1. Practice mindfulness: Mindfulness involves paying attention to the present moment without judgment. This can help you stay grounded and manage negative emotions at the moment.

2. Engage in physical activity: Physical activity can help release tension and reduce stress, making it an effective way to manage negative emotions in the short term.

3. Connect with others: Connecting with others through social support or fun activity can help you feel less isolated and manage negative emotions.

4. Use deep breathing: Deep breathing is a simple yet effective tool for managing stress and negative emotions. Taking a few deep breaths can help you calm down and gain perspective.

Long-term solutions:

1. Develop healthy coping mechanisms: Developing beneficial coping tools, such as journaling or practicing mindfulness, can help

you manage negative emotions in the long term.

2. Address the root cause: Negative emotions often stem from deeper issues, such as past trauma or unmet needs. Addressing the root cause of negative emotions can help you manage them more effectively in the long term.

3. Cultivate gratitude: Focusing on what you are grateful for can help shift your perspective and reduce the impact of negative emotions.

4. Seek professional help: If you are struggling to manage negative emotions, seeking professional help from a therapist or counselor can be helpful.

By utilizing short-term and long-term solutions, you can gain greater control over your negative emotions and find greater peace and happiness.

CHAPTER 5

Implementing and Tracking Habits

Adopting new habits can be challenging, but several strategies can help make the process easier and more effective. Here are a few tips for implementing and tracking your habits:

1. **Use a Habit Tracker** - A habit tracker is a simple tool that can help you keep track of your progress and stay motivated. Habit tracking lets you stay accountable, see your progress over time, and identify patterns hindering your success. You can use a physical planner, an app, or even a simple sheet of paper to track your habits.

2. **Make it a Routine** - Make your new habit part of your daily routine by setting aside a specific time each day to complete it. For example, if you want to start practicing gratitude, set aside time each morning to write down three things you are grateful for.

3. **Start Small** - Starting with small, manageable habits can make the process of habit formation less overwhelming. As you establish the pattern, you can gradually increase the difficulty or frequency as needed.

4. **Find an Accountability Partner** - Having an accountability partner can help you stay

motivated and on track. You can enlist a friend, family member, or even a coach to check in with you regularly and offer encouragement and support.

5. **Celebrate Your Successes** - Celebrating your successes, no matter how small, can help you stay motivated and on track. Whether it's a pat on the back, a treat, or simply acknowledging your progress, taking the time to celebrate your successes can help keep you motivated and focused on your goals.

6. **Be Patient** - Building new habits takes time and effort, and it's essential to be patient with yourself. Remember that change is a process, and setbacks and challenges are a normal part of the journey. Celebrate your progress and stay focused on your goals; you will eventually reach them.

Tracking and implementing your habits is vital to transform your life in 30 days successfully. By following these tips, you can stay motivated and focused and set yourself up for lasting happiness and success.

CHAPTER 6

Overcoming Obstacles

Building new habits can be a challenging process, and it's common to encounter obstacles along the way. Here are some common barriers and strategies for overcoming them:

1. **Lack of Motivation** - It can be challenging to find the motivation to stick with a new habit, especially if it's something you don't enjoy. To overcome this, try to discover why you want to adopt this habit and remind yourself of this reason every time you feel unmotivated. You can also associate the practice with something you enjoy, such as listening to music or reading a book.

2. **Procrastination** - Procrastination can be a significant obstacle to habit formation, and it's essential to take action to overcome it. One strategy is to start small and build up gradually rather than trying to tackle the habit all at once. You can also break the routine into smaller, manageable steps and celebrate each step.

3. **Lack of Time** - Time constraints can make it challenging to adopt new habits, especially if they require a lot of time and effort. To overcome this, prioritize the practice and

make time for it each day. You can also find ways to make the habit more efficient, such as combining it with another activity or delegating other tasks to free up time.

4. **Fear of Failure** - Fear of failure can be a significant obstacle to habit formation, and it's essential to address this fear head-on. To overcome it, focus on the process rather than the outcome and celebrate your successes. You can also find an accountability partner who can support and encourage you and remind you that failure is a natural part of growth.

5. Distractions can be a significant obstacle to habit formation, and taking action to minimize them is vital. To overcome this, try to remove distractions, such as turning off your phone or finding a quiet workplace. You can also plan your day and prioritize your habits so that you can focus on them without distraction.

6. **Old** habits can be challenging to break and often interfere with your efforts to adopt new practices. To overcome this, try to identify the triggers that lead to your old habits and find ways to replace them with new habits. You can also be mindful of your old habits and consciously try to break them.

Overcoming obstacles is an integral part of the habit formation process, and staying focused and committed to your goals is essential. With the right mindset, encouragement, and support, you can successfully transform your life in 30 days.

CHAPTER 7

Reflecting on Progress

Reflecting on progress is a critical part of the habit-forming process, and taking the time to assess your progress after 30 days is essential. This reflection can help you identify areas for improvement, celebrate your successes, and maintain the positive changes you've made throughout the challenge. Here are some suggestions for reflecting on your progress:

1. **Keep a Journal** - Keeping a journal of your journey can help you reflect on your progress and identify areas for improvement. Write down your thoughts and feelings, and reflect on the habits you've adopted and the progress you've made.

2. **Celebrate Your Successes** - Take the time to celebrate your successes, no matter how small they may be. Acknowledge the progress you've made and the habits you've formed, and give yourself credit for your hard work and dedication.

3. **Evaluate Your Habits** - Evaluate each habit you've adopted, and determine whether it's something you'd like to continue or if it's time to move on to a new routine. This evaluation

can help you refine your habits and keep your progress moving forward.

4. **Find an Accountability Partner** - Find someone who can hold you accountable and provide encouragement and support as you continue your habit-forming journey. This person can be a friend, family member, or professional coach.

5. **Set New Goals** - Set new goals for yourself, and continue challenging yourself to grow and improve. This can help you maintain your progress and keep your habit-forming journey moving forward.

6. **Practice Gratitude** - Practice gratitude by focusing on the positive aspects of your life and the progress you've made. This can help you maintain a positive outlook and keep your habit-forming journey moving forward.

By reflecting on your progress, you can stay motivated and on track with your habit-forming journey and continue transforming your life for lasting happiness and success.

CHAPTER 8

Conclusion

In conclusion, "Transform Your Life in 30 Days: Simple Habits for Lasting Happiness and Success" is a guide that encourages readers to take small steps towards lasting change by adopting one new habit per day for 30 days. The book emphasizes the importance of creating positive habits and breaking negative ones and presents a variety of simple habits that can significantly impact happiness and success.

Reflecting on progress is a critical part of the habit-forming process. The book encourages readers to take the time to assess their progress and maintain the positive changes made for the challenge. The book also provides practical tips for implementing and tracking habits and offers strategies for overcoming common obstacles to habit formation.

The key takeaways from the book are that small, consistent changes can lead to significant and lasting transformations in one's life. Habits can shape our lives, and by adopting positive practices and breaking negative ones, we can create a happier and more successful life.

We hope that you have found this 30-day challenge helpful and that you are on your way to transforming your life for lasting happiness and success. Remember to take things one day at a time, and trust that small steps can lead to significant changes. Good luck on your journey, and may you find the happiness and success you deserve!

Study Guide

Transform Your Life in 30 Days: Simple Habits for Lasting Happiness and Success

Chapter 1: Introduction

1. What is the purpose of the book "Transform Your Life in 30 Days"?

The book aims to help readers transform their lives in just 30 days by adopting simple habits that lead to lasting happiness and success.

2. Why is it essential to happiness and success?

Habits play a crucial role in shaping our lives, and developing positive habits can help us lead more fulfilling life. By forming practices that promote happiness and success, we can create a foundation for a better future and experience lasting change.

Chapter 2: The Power of Habits

1. What is the science of habits?

The science of habits refers to studying how habits form, persist, and change over time. It explores the psychological and neurological mechanisms that drive habit formation and how they impact our behavior.

2. Why is it essential to create positive habits and break negative ones?

Creating positive habits and breaking negative ones are essential for leading a happy and successful life. Positive habits help us develop a growth mindset, build resilience, and create a positive impact in our lives. Breaking negative habits can help us overcome self-sabotaging behaviors and improve our mental and emotional well-being.

Chapter 3: The 30-Day Challenge

1. What is the 30-day challenge about?

The 30-day challenge involves adopting one new habit per day for 30 days. This process helps readers create lasting change in their lives by gradually building positive habits and breaking negative ones.

2. How does the 30-day challenge help readers create lasting change in their lives?

The 30-day challenge helps readers create lasting change by allowing them to focus on one habit at a time, which makes the process more manageable and achievable. By gradually incorporating new practices into their lives, readers can build a solid foundation for lasting change and achieve their goals over time.

Chapter 4: Simple Habits for Transformation

1. What are some of the simple habits that can have a significant impact on happiness and success?

Some simple habits that can significantly impact happiness and success include gratitude, exercise, mindfulness, and goal-setting. These habits help promote positive thinking, increase self-awareness, and build resilience, all of which contribute to a happier and more successful life.

Chapter 5: Implementing and Tracking Habits

1. What are some practical tips for implementing and tracking habits?

Some practical tips for implementing and tracking habits include using habit trackers and accountability partners. Tracking habits helps readers stay motivated and on track with their goals, and having an accountability partner can help provide support and encouragement along the way.

Chapter 6: Overcoming Obstacles

1. What are some common obstacles to habit formation?

Common obstacles to habit formation include lack of motivation, accountability, and resistance to change. These obstacles can make it challenging to stick to new habits, but with the right strategies, readers can overcome them and achieve their goals.

Chapter 7: Reflecting on Progress

1. Why is it important to reflect on progress after 30 days?

Reflecting on progress after 30 days is important because it allows readers to evaluate their progress and identify areas for improvement. This process helps readers maintain momentum and build positive habits in the future.

Chapter 8: Conclusion

1. What are the key takeaways from the book "Transform Your Life in 30 Days"?

The key takeaways from the book "Transform Your Life in 30 Days" are the importance of developing positive habits, the power of the 30-day challenge, and the impact that small steps toward lasting change can have on one's life. Readers are encouraged to make the most of the 30-day challenge and embrace the journey toward a happier and more prosperous future.

Thanks for reading; please remember to comment and share with family and friends.

Daily Note and Meditation

1

Take a deep breath in, and imagine yourself surrounded by a warm and comforting light as you exhale.

2

Close your eyes and visualize yourself standing in a beautiful, serene garden. The sun is shining down, warming your skin, and the gentle breeze carries the sweet fragrance of flowers to your nose.

3

Take a deep breath and imagine that you're drawing in peace and calm with each inhale. And with each exhale, you're releasing any stress or tension that may be holding you back.

4

Now, picture a white dove soaring overhead. Watch as it circles in the sky, its wings spread wide and its body at peace. As you watch the dove, imagine yourself becoming more and more relaxed.

5

Visualize a stream of warm, comforting energy flowing through your body, starting at the crown of your head and flowing down to your toes. Feel this energy wash away any worries or negative thoughts, leaving you refreshed and rejuvenated.

6

Take a few deep breaths and when you're ready, slowly open your eyes, feeling relaxed and at peace.

Note After Meditation.

After completing this meditation, it's essential to take a few moments to ground yourself before resuming your daily activities. Here are a few tips to help you do this:

1. **Take a few deep breaths**: Inhale deeply, hold for a moment, and then exhale slowly. Repeat this a few times to help you feel more centered and present.

2. **Move your body**: Stretch your limbs, take a walk, or do a few gentle yoga poses to help you reintegrate into your physical body.

3. **Drink some water**: Meditation can dehydrate you, so make sure to hydrate yourself by drinking water.

4. **Reflect on your experience**: Take a moment to reflect on what you experienced during the meditation. Write down any insights, feelings, or thoughts that came up for you.

5. **Re-engage with your environment**: Gradually re-engage with your surroundings, being mindful of your thoughts and feelings as you do so.

Remember to be kind to yourself, and don't judge any thoughts or emotions that come up after your meditation. The point of reflection is to create awareness and increase your overall sense of well-being, not to suppress or eliminate negative thoughts and feelings.

CPSIA information can be obtained
at www.ICGtesting.com
Printed in the USA
LVHW041756220223
740175LV00033B/760

9 789692 992725